Mina Ballerina

Follow your dreams, not your assumed path.

Copyright 2021 by Cori Nevruz
All rights reserved.
This book or any portion thereof may not be reproduced or used in any manner whatsoever without the express written permission of the author except for the use of brief quotations in a book review.

First Printing, 2021

The ballet came to town
on a crisp autumn night,
and Mina was born
to the dancer's delight.

When Mina grew up,
She would get her big chance.

She practiced her counts,
her positions and poses.

was the work she put in to be the next star.

Rather than dance, she wished to play with their brothers.

Her heart tried to share what her mind couldn't get,

Her hair in a bun on top of her head,

but where her tights went,
long socks were instead.

It was the black lines she drew under her eyes.

Was it the cheers making her braver and bolder?

Her mind worked out what her heart knew all along.

Illustrators

Giada Martucci (12)
Poppy Coleman (13)
Mallory Blackburn (14)
Julia Beveridge (14)
Allie Sauer (10)
Lila Pfirman (13)
Kaylee Appleton (12)
Lilah Rose Heatherly (11)
Sallie Brown (13)
Libby Williamson (10)
Isla Tesch (9)
Anne Wells Lowery (11)
Chloe D. Alimpangog (9)
Eliza Lowery (8)
Kara Appleton (7)
Montana Star Owen (13)
Cate Skiles (14)
Carolina "Carly" Tesch (11)
Abigail W. Zheng (10)
Ella Carpenter (12)
Sophie Gee (11)

www.ingramcontent.com/pod-product-compliance
Lightning Source LLC
Chambersburg PA
CBHW061751290426
44108CB00028B/2961